N is for Nostril

...and other alphabet silliness

written and illustrated by

Joe Spooner

— Joe Spooner
September 2008

For Patti, Norah, John, Papa, Dee Dee, Spike, Polly, Pat, Dan, Ellen, Diane, Neil, Terry, Dave, Pam, Kevin, Lila, Randy, Julie, Sue, Dan, Sharon, Julie, Tim, Robin, Marj, Rick, Patrick, Kevin, Helen, Vince, Phoebe, Patrick, Emily, Tony, Jemie, Mike, Jeff, Georgiana, Bailey, Steve, Nancy, Keith, Gretta, Doug, Carolyn, Joyce, Jerry, Jonathan, Melissa, Jasper, Aviva, Dan, Susan, Hank, Jane, Scott, Cody, Rick, Lily, Peter, Jack, Cathy, Chuck, Lois, Danielle, Jonathan, Chris, John, J.J., Joanna, Jeff, Marcie, Susan, Jim, Earl, Jeanne, Karen, Ethan, Michael, Joel, Julie, Tuomo, Katie, Karl, Susan, Gabe, Garrett, Gabi, Barb, Matthew, Joey, Moni, Henry, Anna, Domi, Pat, Lauren, Michael, Micheline, Joe, Lara, Cobin, Michelle, Joe, Lynn, John, Gail, Barb, Alison, Daniel, Auntie Vi, Josh, Doug, Heidi, Barbara, Gil, Christie, Gil, Christie, Jody, Pat, Reed, Piper, Nicole, John, Connie, Daryl, Cheryl, Smitty, Roselyne, Tim, Marie Claire, J.B., Martha, Morry, John, Cathy, Milton, Jackie, Sara, Thomas, Martin, Julia, Benjamin, Victoria, Lauren, Bill, Barry, Myrna, Jim, Tom, Linda, Jay, David, Barb, Mike, Therese, Michael, Theresa, Alice, John, Mark, Eileen, Cathy, Chuck, Patricia, Bill, Lynn, Terry, Bill, Laurie, Jim, Jo, Tom, Erica, Phil, Mary, Jamie, Casey, Diane, Mr. Bell, Fr. Krall, Bob, Ricky, Jeff, Dan, Ralph, Dave, Fred, Stephen, Peter, Bonnie, Gene, Katie, Smokey, Michelle, Ross, Gloria, Rachael, Aimee, Mattie, Ken, Melva, Troy, Janet, Wendy, Nick, Bob, Cindy, Rhonda, Ellen, Eli, Clara, Steve, Robin, Brent, Adria, Nancy, Randy, Peter, Ann, Jack, Marsha, Cedar, Danah, William, Joan, Guy, Katie, Julie, Mugsy, Rosie (aka Harvy), P.K., Cheryl, Paul, Lindsy, Riley, Tommy, Nana, Jack, Grandpa Spooner, Grandma Spooner, Dorothy, Commander Keller, Mark, Jeff, Rodney, Jack, Dave, Pat, Mel, Helen, Byron, Sandee, Terry, Craig, Jim, Roger, Archie, Gary, Ricky, Steve, Delores, Greg, Jimmy, Frida, Ry, Bruce, Kris, Edward, Sally, Thomas, Ellen, Arthur, Robert, Sam, Penny, Peter, Paul, Steven, Wilbur, Orville, Newt, Howard Richard, Bertha, Tony, Eileen, Roberta, Kiley, Mechila, Maurice, Skidmore, Wizard, Philip, Ben, Trump, Tina, Rich, Patricia, Paul, Philip, Kevin, George, John, Will, Gladys, Ralph, Norton, Lucy, Johnny, Phil, Anna, Doreen, Bill, Hillary, Calvin, Hobbs, Helen, Byron, Vaughan, Teri, Michael, Mark, Dan, Ellis, Richard, Thomas, Charles, Gary, Terry, Craig, Jim, Roger, Archie, Gary, Ricky, Steve, Delores, Greg, Jimmy, Frida, Ry, Bruce, Kris, Edward, Sally, Thomas, Ellen, Arthur, Robert, Nick, Doug, Heidi, Barbara, Gil, Christie, Gil, Christie, Mortimer, Raina, Chris, Homer and Marj

Library of Congress Cataloging-in-Publication Data

Spooner, Joe.
  N is for nostril--and other alphabet silliness / by Joe Spooner.
    p. cm.
  ISBN-13: 978-0-9794771-1-9 (alk. paper)
  ISBN-10: 0-9794771-1-5 (alk. paper)
  1. English language--Alphabet--Juvenile literature. 2. Alphabet books--Juvenile literature. I. Title.

PE1155.S66 2007
428.1--dc22

                    2007021979

Arnica Publishing
3739 SE 8th Avenue, Suite 1 • Portland, OR 97202
Phone: (503) 225-9900 • Fax: (503) 225-9901
www.arnicacreative.com

Arnica books are available at special discounts when purchased in bulk for premiums and sales promotions, as well as for fund-raising or educational use. Special editions or book excerption can also be created for specification. For details, contact the Sales Director at the address above.

the mouse

The mouse that appears throughout this book does so with the permission of Karl P. Whittiker & Associates. Any rebroadcast or use of the mouse by Major League Baseball (even by the Seattle Mariners) is prohibited. (Okay, the Seattle Mariners can use the mouse, but all those other teams can't.) (Not even with permission.)

A

is for
alligator,

high in the sky.

An alligator is basically a crocodile that needs orthodontics. That and the fact that "alligator" comes two letters before "crocodile" in the dictionary are the main differences between the two.

The American alligator is the largest reptile in North America. An adult can reach up to 18 feet in length. Once on the endangered species list, the American alligator now numbers in the millions and lives all across the southeastern United States. Most of them vote by absentee ballot, even in presidential elections.

Alligators make horrible pilots. They are unable to maintain constant airspeed or constant altitude and their instrument crosscheck is atrocious. Also, when they don't actually eat the ground crew, they are quite rude to them.

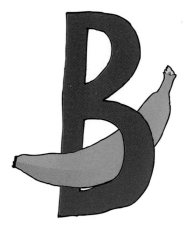

is for
banana,

baked in a pie.

Bananas are almost always sliced up before being put into pies. Some people even go through all the bother of peeling them.

Sir Isaac Newton was under a banana tree when he got his inspiration about gravity. A banana fell on his head and, as he raced off to spread the news about gravity, he slipped on a peel and cracked his head on the ground. The resulting concussion caused him to forget all about his theory. It was another three years before Sir Isaac sat under an apple tree and... well, the rest is history.

Bananas don't actually grow with those little labels on them (not yet, anyway). Those labels are stuck on by humans or robots (see *R is for Robot*).

is for
caterpillar,
asleep in its bed.

Some caterpillars grow to be 2000 times as big as they were when they hatched. If a seven-pound human baby did that, it would weigh over 14,000 pounds when fully grown. But it still wouldn't look much like a giant caterpillar.

The word "caterpillar" was first used in print in 1440. It was spelled catyrpel and meant "hairy cat." People in the 1400s must have had some pretty strange looking cats and they (the people, not the cats) were, most certainly, horryible at spelling.

is for
dachshunds,

pulling a sled.

Dachshunds were bred in Germany and used for hunting badgers. "Dachs" is German for "badger" and "hund" is German for "dog." The dachshund's scientific name, Canis familiaris, is Latin for "wiener dog."

In a 50-yard dash, a dachshund is fast enough to beat the world's fastest human—even without steroids.

The Iditarod is a yearly 1,100-mile dogsled race from Anchorage to Nome, Alaska. It was first run in 1973 and, believe it or not, has NEVER been won by a team of dachshunds.

is for

eggplant,

scrambled or fried.

You can scramble an eggplant. You can sauté or bake it. You can grill it or fry it. It will still taste like an eggplant.

Eggplants arrived in Europe in the eighth century when the Moors invaded Spain. It is surmised (by some very well-educated surmisers) that the Moors used them as weapons.

Doctors at one time thought that eggplants caused fevers and fits. These were the same doctors who also advised their patients to smoke a certain brand of cigarette, to soothe their throats.

is for

fishbowl,

with oatmeal inside.

Did you ever wonder why fish have such low cholesterol? Because they eat oatmeal for breakfast every morning. Yes, every single morning! (If the idea of eating a constant diet of fish food flakes sounds horribly monotonous, try eating oatmeal.)

And while we're on the subject of oatmeal, that one brand, the one with the guy wearing a hat, on a red and blue container? It has no connection with the Religious Society of Friends (Quakers). The name was chosen because of the Quakers' reputation for honesty and dependability and because "Used Car Salesman Oats" seemed a bit too long for a title.

is for

gargoyles,

playing cards on a ledge.

A gargoyle is actually just a waterspout. An ugly, vicious, evil-looking waterspout. If it doesn't spout water, then it's not a gargoyle.

Why do gargoyles sit on building ledges in the first place? Why not darling little cherubs instead? No one knows for sure, but some leading authorities on gargoyles speculate that these stone beasts were placed there to ward off evil. Or maybe to do a more important job: scare away pigeons. But most likely, gargoyles were created to keep gargirls company.

is for
hedgehog,
trimming a hedge.

Hedgehogs are cute little bug-, bee-, worm-, and spider-eating machines. Baby hedgehogs are called hoglets (but certainly not by their mothers). When threatened, a hedgehog rolls itself into a tight ball… just about the right size for a good game of croquet.

When it turns one, the young hedgehog looses its baby spines, which are then replaced by adult spines. Six thousand of them! This, as you can imagine, keeps the spine fairy very, very busy.

is for

igloo,

a really cool home.

An igloo (the Inuit word for "house") is a small, domed structure made out of blocks of snow. The melting and refreezing of the snow blocks creates a smooth, airtight, icy surface and makes the igloo extremely durable. Its interior is heated and lit, traditionally, by a seal-fat lamp. (Seals are not too crazy about this, but it is a good way to lose fat.)

An igloo can be built in three or four hours but the permit process and the environmental-impact studies take up to several months to complete.

One of the most popular shows on Inuit public television is "This Old Igloo."

is for

jellyfish,

using a comb.

The jellyfish, a distant cousin of the marmaladefish, is technically not even a fish. It is an invertebrate in the phylum Cnidaria. Whatever that means.

Most jellyfish are composed of a bell-shaped structure and a set of tentacles covered by stinging cells known (by over-educated, geeky marine biologists) as cnidocytes, and ouchy things by the rest of us. (Okay, maybe marine biologists aren't "geeky.")

A group of jellyfish is called a "smack." And a big smack (available at some fast-food restaurants for $1.29) is called a "bloom."

K

is for
kennel,
a motel for dogs.

The word "kennel" comes from the Latin word cannis, which means (are you ready for this?) "dog." A kennel is a boarding house for dogs.

When boarding your dog at a kennel make sure that he or she has:

- a clean pair of pajamas and a bathrobe
- a dog collar (dog tie is optional)
- a credit card (but with not too big a credit limit... some dogs go crazy at these places—mud baths, dog treats, mud baths, chew toys and mud baths).

is for
ladybug,
cleaning out clogs.

Ladybugs are also known as "lady beetles" and "ladybird beetles." Not all ladybugs are female: some of them are actually gentlemanbugs.

Ladybugs eat aphids. Lots of aphids. A single ladybug can eat as many as 600 aphids in its lifetime. Put chocolate or peanut butter on those aphids and that number really goes up.

Ladybugs are brightly colored and their natural protection is that they taste awful. (If you ate aphids all day long, how do you think you'd taste?)

is for

Martians,

zipping through space.

Martians are an extremely advanced civilization. They were zipping through space while we were still figuring out the wheel.

But for all of their intelligence, Martians have absolutely no sense of direction. None. Martians need a map and compass (and sometimes, cookie crumbs) to go to their next-door neighbor's and back. Which explains why they've never come here. Martians can see Earth in their telescopes and have calculated the complex trajectories to get here. But every time they send a Martianed expedition, it winds up on Mercury or Venus or Pluto (which, by the way, Martians have known for years wasn't a real planet).

Most of the Martians you see in movies and on television are actually heavily made-up Venutians.

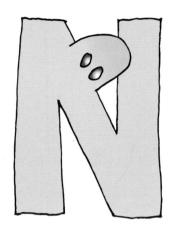 is for

nostrils,

there are two on your face.

"Nostril" comes from two Old English words meaning "nose" and "hole." Who would have guessed?

There are two nostrils per nose. "Why two?" you ask. Because one nostril smells things differently than the other, but I can't remember which one.

Whales and dolphins have just one nostril instead of two and it's on the top of their heads. Their single nostril is called a "blowhole."

Sitting next to a dolphin or a whale when it sneezes is not a very pleasant experience. Especially if you don't have a kleenex with you the size of a bed sheet.

is for

ogre,

crouched under a bridge.

An ogre and a troll are the same thing, except that one of them is Scandinavian and the other one isn't.

The ogre of fairy tales was portrayed as a man-eating, woman-eating, goat-eating monster. But today's ogres are sensitive, caring creatures. Many of them are vegetarians.

Contrary to popular belief, ogres are not stupid. They are actually quite intelligent and make excellent game-show contestants. An ogre recently won $82,000 for knowing the entire second stanza of "The Battle Hymn of the Republic." In French!

is for

pirate,

raiding the fridge.

Pirates are immoral, foul, dishonorable and corrupt reprobates. They aren't very nice either. When they are not plundering and looting ships, pirates are busy copying movies and software and selling them on the Internet.

Pirates have extremely poor diets. Some live for months at a time on nothing but corn dogs and cola drinks. The closest thing to a vegetable they eat is mustard.

is for

quacker,

a saltine or duck.

A saltine cracker (pronounced "quacker" when your mouth is full of them) has holes in it to let steam escape during baking. This keeps the cracker from getting soggy and makes them easier to add to charm bracelets.

The other quacker, a duck, is a member of the Anatidae family. Ducks are called ducks because they "duck" into the water.

Famous ducks include Donald, Daffy, and Howard the. Each of their last names is Duck, yet none of them are related!

is for

robot,

driving a truck.

The term "robot" wasn't used until 1924, and then it was used several times.

Robots today can be programmed to do some fairly complicated tasks, but most of them perform monotonous, repetitive, assembly-line jobs like building cars, putting lids on jars and doing root canals.

Robots often appear in movies — especially in science-fiction movies — but no robot has ever won an acting award. (John Wayne, technically not a robot, did win an award once for best actor.)

is for

scarecrow,

keeping the score.

A group of crows is called a "murder." A group of scarecrows is called "a group of scarecrows."

Crows are excellent bowlers but have a tendency to cheat on their scores. Scarecrows, when they're not standing around in farmers' fields scaring crows (for less than minimum wage), are more than happy to keep score for them (the crows, not the farmers, that is. Farmers can keep score for themselves).

Never offer a scarecrow a cola drink or a milkshake with a straw in it. Scarecrows have no sense of humor and will be deeply offended.

is for

toupee,

worn by a boar.

Wigs have been around almost as long as comb-overs have been. Ancient Egyptians shaved their heads and rich Egyptians wore elaborate wigs made of human hair, sheep's wool or palm-leaf fiber. Poor Egyptians wore hats.

A toupee is a little wig and the word means, "tuft of hair." Toupees came into fashion in the 18th century and used to be single curls or locks of fake hair. Or real hair. But not the "real" hair of the person who has it on. A toupee is designed to appear "natural" only to the person who is wearing it.

is for

uvula,

that thing in your throat.

Mammals (including humans), alligators and crocodiles all have uvulas. A uvula is that silly thing that hangs down at the back of the roof of your mouth.

Its main purpose is to vibrate back and forth in the wide-open mouth of a singing cartoon character. It also helps to keep food out of your lungs, which prevents you from choking, wheezing, coughing and turning blue when you eat. If you are inhaling your food, your uvula isn't doing its job very well.

is for
varmint,
paddling a boat.

Varmint is a variation on the word "vermin." Vermin are pests—rats, cockroaches, telemarketers—that are annoying and (except for the telemarketers) tend to destroy crops and property. Varmints are pests that are also predators—coyotes, foxes, and telemarketers. They prey on farm animals and sometimes want to know (usually at dinner time) if you would like to get some magazine subscriptions at extremely good rates.

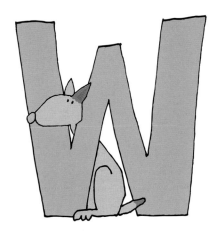

is for

watchdog,

who watches and groans.

A watchdog is an organic home security system, and you don't have to punch in any numbers to turn your watchdog on or off. But then again, if you have an electronic home security system, you don't have to watch every step you take in your backyard.

Dogs have been living with humans longer than any other animal. They were first domesticated to be used as watchdogs: to bark insanely when a saber-toothed tiger or... or a bear, a big scary bear, approached. Now, they warn us, in the same manner, of an approaching... mailman!

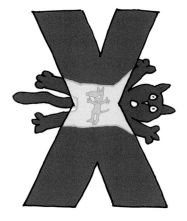

is for

x-ray,

to peek at your bones.

Machines that make x-rays are extremely complicated. To simplify how they work: you turn the switch on and—this part is very cool—you can see all your bones and the cavities in your teeth.

In the past, some super heroes used x-ray vision to see through buildings and walls (and occasionally to make sure that everyone was wearing underpants). Now, most super heroes use CAT-scan vision.

is for

yetis,

who play in the snow.

Yeti, another name for the abominable snowman, is a hairy, man-like (and woman-like) creature that some folks believe lives high in the Himalayan Mountains of Asia. Yetis are first cousins (on their mothers' side) to Bigfoot.

Four thousand years ago, Yetis invented skiing, but they have yet to figure out how to use lift tickets. They are intelligent creatures, but are almost completely uneducated: every year their school year is entirely wiped out by snow days.

is for

zebras

in stripedy clothes.

Belonging to the same class of animals as horses, rhinoceroses and tapirs, the zebra is called a perissodactyla, which means "odd-toed."

Zebras have never been domesticated because they are disagreeable and mean. How would you feel if everyone called you "odd-toed"?

Animals that are plaid do not hang around with zebras because they tend to clash.

Zebras are very family-oriented. They protect one another when attacked and they always schedule meal times together, even on soccer night.